WATCH ANIMALS GROW

Puppies

by Colleen Sexton

BELLWETHER MEDIA • MINNEAPOLIS, MN

Note to Librarians, Teachers, and Parents:

Blastoff! Readers are carefully developed by literacy experts and combine standards-based content with developmentally appropriate text.

Level 1 provides the most support through repetition of high-frequency words, light text, predictable sentence patterns, and strong visual support.

Level 2 offers early readers a bit more challenge through varied simple sentences, increased text load, and less repetition of high-frequency words.

Level 3 advances early-fluent readers toward fluency through increased text and concept load, less reliance on visuals, longer sentences, and more literary language.

Level 4 builds reading stamina by providing more text per page, increased use of punctuation, greater variation in sentence patterns, and increasingly challenging vocabulary.

Level 5 encourages children to move from "learning to read" to "reading to learn" by providing even more text, varied writing styles, and less familiar topics.

Whichever book is right for your reader, Blastoff! Readers are the perfect books to build confidence and encourage a love of reading that will last a lifetime!

This edition first published in 2008 by Bellwether Media.

No part of this publication may be reproduced in whole or in part without written permission of the publisher. For information regarding permission, write to Bellwether Media Inc., Attention: Permissions Department, Post Office Box 19349, Minneapolis, MN 55419.

Library of Congress Cataloging-in-Publication Data
Sexton, Colleen A., 1967–
 Puppies / by Colleen Sexton.
  p. cm. – (Blastoff! Readers: Watch animals grow)
Summary: "A basic introduction to puppies. Simple text and full color photographs. Developed by literacy experts for students in kindergarten through third grade"–Provided by publisher.
 Includes bibliographical references and index.
 ISBN-13: 978-1-60014-170-6 (hardcover : alk. paper)
 ISBN-10: 1-60014-170-6 (hardcover : alk. paper)
 1. Puppies–Juvenile literature. I. Title.

SF426.5.S49 2008
636.7'07–dc22   2007040275

Contents

A mother dog
gives birth to
puppies.
She **licks** the
puppies. They
start to breathe.

Newborn puppies cannot see or hear. They can smell their mother. They stay close to their mother.

Puppies drink milk from their mother. Milk helps puppies grow strong.

Puppies grow quickly. Soon they open their eyes.

Puppies grow
teeth. Now
they can eat
puppy food.

Puppies bite and **chew** to clean their teeth.

Puppies run
and play.

Puppies sleep
a lot. Sleeping
helps them grow.

19

Puppies can leave their mother after eight weeks. This happy puppy has a new home!

Glossary

chew—to crush and grind with teeth; chewing on toys helps dogs keep their teeth clean and strong.

lick—to wipe with the tongue; mother dogs lick their newborn puppies to clean them and help them breathe.

puppy food—food for puppies; puppy food is made from meat, grains, and vegetables.

To Learn More

AT THE LIBRARY
Dolbear, Emily J., and E. Russell Primm. *Dogs Have Puppies*. Minneapolis, Minn.: Compass Point Books, 2001.

Ganeri, Anita. *From Puppy to Dog*. Chicago, Ill.: Heinemann, 2006.

Grogan, John. *Bad Dog, Marley!* New York: HarperCollins, 2007.

ON THE WEB
Learning more about puppies is as easy as 1, 2, 3.

1. Go to www.factsurfer.com

2. Enter "puppies" into search box.

3. Click the "Surf" button and you will see a list of related web sites.

With factsurfer.com, finding more information is just a click away.

Index

The images in this book are reproduced through the courtesy of: Brian Sytnyk/Masterfile, front cover; Juniors Bildarchiv/Alamy, p. 5; Hannamariah, p. 7; Stephen Coburn, p. 9; Scott Tysick/Masterfile, p. 11; Petra Wegner/Alamy, p. 13; Arthur Tilley/Getty Images, p. 15; Joy Fera, p. 17; SuperStock/Age fotostock, p. 19; ARCO/C. Roy Morsch/Age fotostock, p. 21.